Lively Limericks

Lively Limericks

Ribald Rhymes and Saucy Verses

Collected and contributed by
Patrick Holden

illustrated by
Oliver Preston and Bill Stott

First published in Great Britain in 2015 by
BEVERSTON PRESS
Tetbury, Glos GL8 8TT

British Library cataloguing in Publication Data
A catalogue record for this title is available from The British
Library

ISBN 978-0-9549936-6-5

Designed by boinggraphics.co.uk
Printed by Gutenberg Press, Malta

There is an old limericist who
Decided that nothing's taboo;
His words are so rude
His verses so lewd
I'm sure they'll appeal to you!

Some are old, some are new,
Some are borrowed, some are blue.

Patrick Holden

Ungracious

I sat next to the Duchess at tea;
It was just as I feared it would be -
Her rumblings abdominal
Were truly phenomenal
And everyone thought it was me!

More Ungracious

When I sat next to the Duchess at tea
She asked "Do you fart when you pee?"
I said: "Not a bit!
Do you belch when you shit?"
And felt it was one up to me ...

OLIVER PRESTON

Disgrace

There once was a toothless old Duke
Who of consommé only partook;
His son, with a scowl
Cried "This fare is foul -
Too many broths spoil the cook!"

More Disgrace

When the Duke took a turn for the worse,
His hopeful heir ordered a hearse;
His Grace, with a grin,
Called Nurse Nightingale in:
The Duke then took a turn for the nurse!

OLIVER PRESTON

Milk Bar

There was a young lady called Pat
Who had triplets, called Nat, Tat and Hat.
With Nat on her east breast
And young Hat on her west,
There was, alas, no tit for Tat.

Another Odd One Out:

There was a young girl from Devizes
Whose boobs were of different sizes;
One was so small
It was no use at all,
But the other won several first prizes.

Scatological?

There was a young plumber from Ryde
Who fell into a privy and died;
The next day his brother
Fell into another
And now they're interred side by side.

Don't look up

Round London the pigeons fly high
And they shit like a shot in your eye.
Although we all curse,
It will be much worse
When elephants learn how to fly!

Never say Never

There was an old spinster, Lavinia
Who was ravished by crooks in Sardinia;
She succumbed to their charms
Then swooned in their arms,
Crying "Darlings, I've simply forgiven 'ya."

In Gallia Veritas

There was a young hooker called Ruth
A striver and seeker of truth;
This pretty young wench
Was adept at French
And said that all else was uncouth.

Ad-vantage

On her boobs a hooker called Gail
Had tattooed the price of each sale;
Whilst on her behind,
For the sake of the blind,
She'd exactly the same but in Braille.

Sewing, not reaping

Said a fertile young father from Tyne,
"That's it, enough's enough, eight's fine,
Now a vasectomy
Seems correct to me -
As they say 'A stitch in time saves nine.'"

Planning Consent

There was a young lady of Wantage
Of whom the Town Clerk took advantage;
"Indeed you must pay her,"
Said the Borough Surveyor,
"You've totally altered her frontage."

Unplanned Consent

There was a young lady from Louth
Who returned from a jaunt to the South;
Her father said "Nelly
There's more in your belly
Than ever went in by your mouth."

Trigamy

There was a young lawyer of Lyme
Who married three wives at one time.
When asked "Why a third?"
He replied, "One's absurd,
And bigamy, sir, is a crime."

Very PC

There was a young lassie called Dee
Who trained hard to become a PC;
She found Drugs were nice
Then succeeded in Vice
And now is DCI, CID

Burning Issues

There was a young libber from Tottenham
Who'd no scruples or else she'd forgotten 'em;
One day at her Ma's
She lit both their bras -
It's no wonder they felt so hot in 'em!

One Strike Down

When the Bermondsey bricklayers struck,
'Arry 'Awkins was 'aving a f***;
By union rules
'E 'ad to down tools -
Now wasn't that 'ard bleedin' luck?

Perfidious Albion

In matters moral we Brits are absurd -
See our use of the four letter word:
We can have sex, with luck,
But not rhyme it with 'duck' -
Thus we may be obscene, but not heard.

NOT Jam & Jerusalem

A young matron of the W.I.,
Tired of motherhood and apple pie,
Proposed an agenda
Of a nudist calendar
Showing everyone's bum, boobs and thigh.

Failed Intent

There was a young couple from Kent
Who tried to have sex in a tent;
The wind kept blowing,
Soon it was snowing,
So rather than coming, they went.

Uni-verse

A graduate known as Louise
Was loaded with MA's and DD's;
She collapsed from the weight
Of diplomas so great -
She was killing herself by degrees.

A nubile young lass from St. Paul
Who undressed at every May Ball
Was a corking success
With the opposite sex -
The good time who was had by all.

A divine girl

A maudlin don of Divinity
Had a daughter who kept her virginity;
The Fellows at Magdalene
Were obviously daudling -
It could never have happened at Trinity.

That maudlin don of Divinity
Then lost his young daughter to Trinity;
He took to free thinking
And then to deep drinking:
The Dean made him quit the vicinity.

Ice Maiden

There was a young girl whose frigidity
Approached cataleptic rigidity,
'Til you gave her a drink,
When she quickly would sink
In a state of complacent liquidity.

Physician's Coition Tuition Fruition

There was a young lady called Brigid
Who wanted to stop being frigid;
Her physician's tuition
Brought coition fruition
When he screwed frigid Brigid rigid.

OLIVER PRESTON

One That Got Away

There was a young fellow named Fisher
Who was fishing for fish in a fissure;
Then a fish with a grin,
Pulled the fisherman in -
Now they're fishing the fissure for Fisher.

Bare-faced Cheek

I met a young nude in Bermuda
Who thought she was shrewd; I was shrewder.
To her it seemed crude
To be wooed in the nude.
I pursued her, subdued her and screwed her.

OLIVER PRESTON

More Bare Faced Cheek

There was a young lady called Clare
Who ran through the market all bare;
"Ignorance!" they tasked -
"Apathy?" they asked:
Cried she, "I don't know, and I don't care."

OLIVER PRESTON

Best Seller

A publisher once went to France
In search of a tale of romance.
A Parisian lady
Told a story so shady,
That the publisher made an advance.

Mixed Views

There was a young person called Glenda
Who was oddly uncertain of gender;
For a tenner or two
She would let the world view
His astonishing double pudenda.

Pink Lady

There was a young lady from Ryde
Who ate green apples and died.
The apples fermented
Inside the lamented
And made cider inside her inside.

Blossoming talent

A geneticist living in Leeds
Once swallowed some GM seeds;
In well under an hour
His prick was a flower
And his buttocks kept sprouting new weeds.

OLIVER PRESTON

Chivalry

There was a brave knight called Sir Lancelot
Who liked, after jousting, to dance a lot;
A loving "My dear come here"
From his Queen, Guinevere,
Made Lancelot's own lance advance a lot.

Love bite?

A vampirous Duke from Sylvania
Fancied a girl called Titania;
To humour his lust
He bit on her bust -
And gave her bad nymphomania.

OLIVER PRESTON

Wherefore Art thou?

A young Norman lady called Pru,
Her chastity belt locked with glue,
Was bored by her warder
Who simply adored her;
Her lock was thus picked by a screw.

There was a young lady from York,
Who thought she'd be safe with a cork;
Her man took a view
Then used a corkscrew -
And now she's expecting the stork.

Fartistry

A flatulent conductor called Bart
Was encored for original art;
You might think it sordid
But his hearers applauded
That regular rhythmical fart.

Double Decker

There was a nude bimbo from Ham
Who rashly jumped onto a tram.
When once she'd embarked,
The conductor remarked,
"Your fare, miss?" She lisped, "Yeth, I am."

Said the Dean in her actress's class,
"Speak clearly: you must roll your r's."
"Sir," she said in reply,
"To speak clearly, I'll try,
But why must I waggle my arse?"

Paternal advice

"Son," his father said, "You're a rake.
Settle down for your family's sake.
Change your dissolute life,
And take yourself a wife."
"Yes Dad , whose wife shall I take?"

Young shaver?

If you catch a chinchilla in Chile
And cut off its beard, willy-nilly
With a small razor blade,
You can say that you've made
A Chile Chinchilla's chin chilly.

Riga mortis?

There was a young lady from Riga
Who smiled as she rode on a tiger;
They came back from that ride,
With the lady inside
And the smile on the face of the tiger.

An All-time Great

While Titian was mixing rose madder,
His model posed nude on a ladder:
Her position to Titian,
Suggested coition
So he leapt up the ladder and 'ad her.

OLIVER PRESTON

Cambridge Classic

There was a young gourmet of John's,
Who'd a notion of dining on swans;
To the Backs he took big nets,
To entrap some cygnets
But was told they were kept for the dons.

Classic update

There was a young student of John's
Who tried to roger the swans.
"Oh, Sir," cried the Porter
"You can have my daughter,
But the swans are reserved for the dons."

A Trick Cyclist

That transvestite painter van Eyck
Travelled around Holland by bike;
While pushing his passion
For cross-dressing fashion
His finger got stuck in a dyke.

OLIVER PRESTON

Bombastic

There was a young genius at Queen's
Who was fond of exploding machines;
Once he blew up a door
But he'll do it no more
For it chanced that the door was the Dean's.

At Harvard there was an old Dean
Who invented a f***ing machine;
Concave or convex
It would fit either sex,
And was remarkably easy to clean.

Classic

There was a young plumber from Leigh
Who was plumbing his girl by the sea
Said she "Someone's coming!"
Said the plumber, still plumbing,
"If anyone's coming it's me!"

There was a young lady of Leigh
Who stood on her head in the sea:
Her immersion inversion
Suggested perversion
When her legs were splayed out in a 'V'.

Honi soit ....

There once was a lass from Madras
Who had a magnificent ass;
Not firm, round and pink
As *you* probably think -
It was grey, had long ears and ate grass.

Revealing

There was a young lady from Ealing
Who performed a striptease so appealing,
Not a whisper was heard,
Not a sound, not a word –
Only flybuttons hitting the ceiling!

There was a young lady of Norway
Who hung by her heels from a doorway;
To her lover she said
"Darling, get out of bed -
I think I've discovered one more way!"

Re-Volt

That lean lethargic layabout Lance,
Really couldn't be bothered to dance
Til' a lightning bolt
Gave his butt a jolt;
Lance now jives with amps in his pants.

Decline and fall?

Till thirty a man is proficient,
At forty he's fairly efficient;
But by fifty and nine
He's begun to decline -
And at ninety he's only deficient.

At eighty some men are still heels
As they chase girls with zimmers on wheels;
They don't often feel lonely -
As they say "Man is only
As old as the woman he feels."

The enjoyment of sex although great
Is said in late years to abate;
That may well be so
But how would I know ?
I am only one hundred and eight!

Fin-ished

There was a young bather called Mark
Who saw the fin of a white shark
He said, "The deep sea
Is no place for me,
I'll swim in the lake in the park".

Fin-ished Off

That same young bather called Mark
When he went to the loo in the dark;
Imagine his shock,
When he saw in that crock,
The fin of that great white shark.

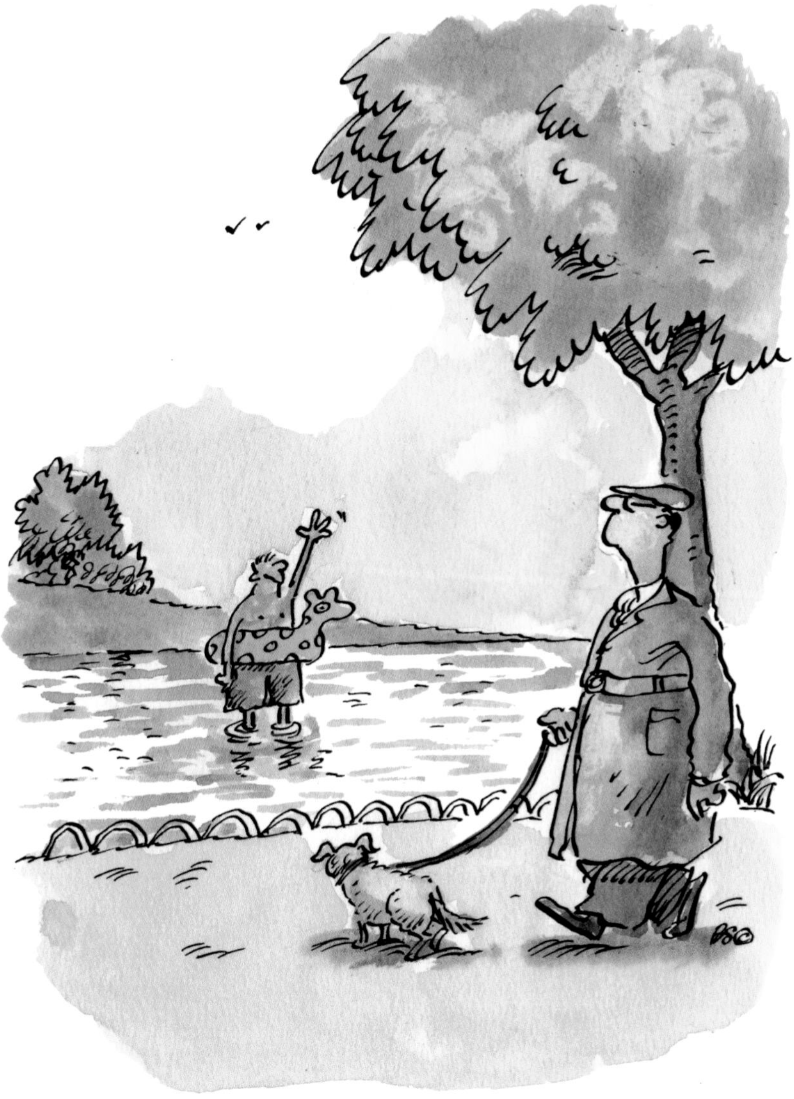

Getting First Aida?

Said Guiseppe Verdi to a fan
"After many drinks with the barman,
Composing's OK;
Like my dear friend, Bizet,
I don't know if I'm going or Carmen."

True Professionals?

At the end of a trial, a court visitor
Asked the Judge, "Please elicit or
Explain why it's illicit
For a girl to solicit,
But lawful to be a solicitor."

OLIVER
PRESTON.

Philosophical Hot Air

Said Lord Russell one day by the Cam
"We philosophers don't give a damn:
Whenever I fart,
I agree with Descartes
When he said 'I stink therefore, I am.' "

A Cautionary Tale

There was a young cannibal called Ned
Who used to eat garlic in bed.
Cried his mum, "Can't you tell
That this veg makes you smell?
Why don't you eat people instead?"

So that cannibal Ned of Penzance
Ate an uncle and two of his aunts
A cow and her calf,
An ox and a half,
And now he can't button his pants.

Hot Gospel or Cook's Tour

A cannibal bold from Timbuktu
Said "Tourists? We've just cooked two;
One was short fat and hairy,
The other was a missionary
We stewed him, cassock and hymn book too."

C.looless

There was a young person called Fred
Who decided to paint the town red;
Though he felt rather blue
When he'd trashed the town's loo -
Crying "There is no pees for the wicked".

Insect Inside

Said a flea to a fly in a flue,
"We're prisoners - what can we do?"
"Let us flee," said the fly.
"Let us fly," said the flea.
So they flew through a flaw in the flue.

Ahoy!

There was a young sailor called Sue
Who slept with each one of the crew
Not from ocean emotion
But her own naive notion
That the ship was propelled by a screw.

The crew all remembered to thank her
And Sue slept, while the ship rode at anchor.
She awoke with dismay
To hear the mate say
"Men, pull up the top sheet and spanker."